WHO WOULD WIN?®

ULTIMATE REPTILE RUMBLE

BY
JERRY PALLOTTA

ILLUSTRATED BY
ROB BOLSTER

Scholastic Inc.

*The publisher would like to thank the following for their
kind permission to use their photographs in this book:*
Photos ©: 2 background: G-ZStudio/Shutterstock; 3 crocodile: Aoosthuizen/Getty Images;
5: Miles Barton/Minden Pictures; 16: MollyNZ/Getty Images; 17 top: Susan Schmitz/Shutterstoc
19 top: IrinaK/Shutterstock; 32 gavial: Science & Society Picture Library/Getty Images.

REPTILE BRACKET

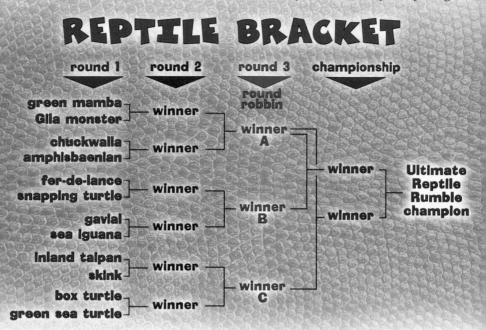

| round 1 | round 2 | round 3 | championship |

green mamba
Gila monster — winner

chuckwalla
amphisbaenian — winner

round robbin

winner A

fer-de-lance
snapping turtle — winner

gavial
sea iguana — winner

winner B

inland taipan
skink — winner

box turtle
green sea turtle — winner

winner C

winner

winner

**Ultimate
Reptile
Rumble
champion**

Welcome Reece Robert Robinson, Claire Elizabeth Pallotta, and Brett Owens Dellelo!
—J.P.

For cousins, Quinn, Camden, Callen, Donovan, and Mattie Grace.
—R.B.

Text copyright © 2021 by Jerry Pallotta
Illustrations copyright © 2021 by Rob Bolster

ISBN 978-1-338-67216-9

10 9 8 7 6 5 4
22 23 24 25

Printed in the U.S.A.
First printing, 2021

40

Welcome to the Ultimate Reptile Rumble! Twelve fierce reptiles are going to battle it out. Who do you think will win?

SALTWATER CROCODILE

DID YOU KNOW?
Saltwater crocodiles can weigh a ton. They can be 20 feet long.

MATH FACT
One ton is 2,000 pounds.

NAME FACT
They are nicknamed "Saltie."

It is simple: If we allow the saltwater crocodile in this book, it will win the competition. This ferocious creature is the largest reptile in the world. It can swim fast, jump completely out of the water, and move quickly on land. Look at that mouth! We will save it for another time.

LEATHERBACK TURTLE

Crocodiles, alligators, turtles, snakes, lizards, amphisbaenians, and tuatara are in a group of animals called reptiles. Scientists call them Reptilia.

DIGGING FACT
Amphisbaenians are burrowing reptiles.

LIVING FOSSIL
The tuatara is the only living rhynchocephalian—all the others are extinct.

DID YOU KNOW?
Reptiles are cold-blooded.

The leatherback sea turtle is the largest turtle in the world, weighing up to 1,500 pounds! It is not fair for it to fight a small lizard or a small snake. Sorry, leatherback sea turtle, you cannot be in this competition.

RETICULATED PYTHON

The longest snake in the world is the reticulated python. It is simply too long for this bracketed battle. How could it ever fight a flowerpot snake that is as small as your little finger?

FACT
A reticulated python grows to be 25 feet long. That's about as long as a school bus!

FACT
Reptiles have dry, scaly skin.

DID YOU KNOW?
The heaviest snake in the world is the green anaconda.

KOMODO DRAGON

The Komodo dragon is the largest lizard on earth. Don't be greedy, Komodo dragon, you already have your own book. At ten feet long, you are too big. Sorry! You are not welcome in the *Ultimate Reptile Rumble* competition.

> **FACT**
> *Komodo dragons have mouths full of dangerous bacteria. They also have blood thinners in their saliva.*

> **FUN FACT**
> *The study of reptiles is called* herpetology.

That's it: The saltwater crocodile, leatherback turtle, reticulated python, and Komodo dragon are out! Goodbye! Now, on to the rumble!

Let the show begin. Our first fight in this competition is a green mamba versus a Gila monster. When a reptile loses, it is out of the contest. The green mamba is a venomous snake.

ROUND 1 — GREEN MAMBA VS. GILA MONSTER — MATCH 1

Only a few lizards in the world are venomous. The Gila monster is one of them. Gila monsters live most of their lives underground.

Both reptiles decide to get some sun. The green mamba comes down from the shade of a tree as the Gila monster climbs out of its underground burrow. The snake spots the lizard.

The Gila monster is slow and no match for the shifty green mamba. The green mamba immediately attacks and bites the Gila monster, injecting it with venom. The fight is over.

GREEN MAMBA WINS!

POISON FACT
Some venom affects your nerves.
Other venom damages your heart.

The chuckwalla is a lizard with a very clever defensive behavior. When threatened, it crawls into a crack in a rock and expands its body. It blows up like a balloon. This makes it impossible to wrestle out of a crevice.

ROUND 1 — CHUCKWALLA VS. AMPHISBAENIAN — MATCH 2

The next fight features an amphisbaenian. Everyone has heard of snakes, crocodiles, and lizards, but amphisbaenians get no respect or publicity. Not many people know about them.

The amphisbaenian tries to bite the lizard. The chuckwalla fights back. The chuckwalla's legs give it an advantage. It bounces around and bites the amphisbaenian in the head and neck. The fight is over.

CHUCKWALLA WINS!

CONFUSING
An amphibian is not a reptile. Amphibians are frogs, toads, salamanders, caecilians, and newts.

RESEARCH AND LEARN
Learn the difference between an amphibian and an amphisbaenian.

The fer-de-lance is one of the deadliest snakes on Earth. Yikes! They have extra-long fangs. When they bite, they inject a large amount of venom into their victim. Humans need to totally avoid the fer-de-lance.

MOUTH FACT
Snakes do not chew their food. They only eat things they can swallow whole.

ROUND **1** MATCH **3**

FER-DE-LANCE VS. SNAPPING TURTLE

A snapping turtle has a powerful jaw. Its bite hurts! Some turtles can completely hide in their shells, but a snapping turtle cannot pull itself all the way in.

FACT
An alligator snapping turtle is the largest snapping turtle.

JAW FACT
Turtles do not have teeth.

The snapping turtle is too big for the fer-de-lance to swallow, so it should have no interest in the turtle. Uh-oh! The turtle gets too close. The fer-de-lance is an aggressive snake.

HEAT FACT
The fer-de-lance is a pit viper. It has organs called pits in front of its eyes. This snake can sense your body heat.

The fer-de-lance bites the snapping turtle in the neck. It happens too fast for the turtle to respond. The venom affects the snapping turtle's nerves. The turtle has trouble walking. Then the turtle stops breathing.

FER-DE-LANCE WINS!

A gavial is a crocodile-type reptile with a sword-shaped snout. Its mouth is perfect for catching fish.

FACT
A gavial, or gharial, is also called a fish-eating crocodile.

ROUND 1

GAVIAL VS. SEA IGUANA

MATCH 4

When people see an iguana, they think of a dinosaur. Dinosaurs probably looked a lot like iguanas. They have long tails. There are land iguanas and sea iguanas. This sea iguana lives in the Galápagos Islands.

FACT
The sea iguana eats seaweed.

HISTORY FACT
The iguanodon was the second dinosaur ever discovered. It was named after the iguana.

The gavial's teeth are much longer than the iguana's teeth. The gavial has a stronger tail. They fight, a bite here, a bite there. They wrestle from the land to the water. Chomp! Chomp! Snap!

If you wrote this book, would you say the gavial has a sword-shaped head, an I-shaped head, or a scissor-shaped head?

GAVIAL WINS!

GECKO

OK. Time to take a break. We thought about putting a gecko in the fight bracket, but geckos are too small for this book. Look! Geckos are very colorful. They should be in a color pageant, not a fight.

FACT
Geckos are lizards.

WOW! There are about 1,500 different species of geckos.

DID YOU KNOW?
Some geckos can walk upside down on glass surfaces.

TUATARA

This reptile is too special to be in a battle. Tuatara, don't get hurt! You are a living fossil! This reptile looks like a lizard, but it is from a group of mostly extinct reptiles called Rhynchocephalia.

STRANGE FACT
Tuataras have a third eye on the top of their skull. Scientists think it is used to regulate body heat.

GEOGRAPHIC FACT
Tuataras live only on islands off of New Zealand.

third eye

WORLD MAP

New Zealand

Rhynchocephalia fossils have been found that are more than 200 million years old. Their ancestors lived with dinosaurs.

Back to the tournament! The inland taipan is considered one of the deadliest snakes on earth. It is also rare. It lives in the desert of central Australia.

> **YIKES!**
> *One inland taipan bite has enough venom to kill 100 people.*

> **FUN FACT**
> *A snake can flick its tongue without opening its mouth. The tongue is hidden in a sheath.*

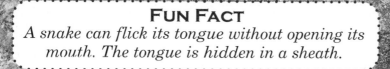

INLAND TAIPAN VS. SKINK

ROUND **1**

MATCH **5**

> **COLOR FACT**
> *The blue tongue helps scare predators away.*

Skinks are burrowing lizards. They prefer to be underground. In this book we are using the blue-tongued skink. They don't like to let go after they bite.

The inland taipan moves across the ground. The skink sneaks up from an underground tunnel and bites the snake. The blue-tongued skink didn't bite a vital spot. The snake turns around and bites and injects venom into the blue-tongued skink.

INLAND TAIPAN FACT
It is also called a fierce snake. It has fierce venom, not a fierce personality.

The venom takes only 30 seconds to work. The skink stops moving.

NICKNAME FACT
This skink is also called "Bluey."

INLAND TAIPAN WINS!

The inland taipan is moving to the next round.

These turtles are called box turtles because they can pull their tail, legs, and head into their shells and be closed in like a box. If you live in North America, you might find one in your neighborhood.

AGE FACT
A box turtle can live to be 100 years old.

HEAT FACT
To warm up, a reptile goes outside and basks in the sun.

The box turtle can swim but it prefers to walk on land. It is a terrestrial turtle.

DEFINITION
Terrestrial means on the Earth.

BOX TURTLE VS. GREEN SEA TURTLE

ROUND **1**

MATCH **6**

This is a green sea turtle. Sea turtles cannot walk on land, but they are great swimmers. These turtles spend their whole lives in the ocean. They come ashore only to lay their eggs.

WET FACT
An aquatic animal lives in the water.

It would be almost impossible for these two turtles to meet in the wild.

A green sea turtle is much larger than a box turtle. If they were the same size, the green sea turtle would have an advantage in water.

The box turtle takes one look at the giant green sea turtle and closes itself inside its box shell. It refuses to come out. The box turtle forfeits the match.

GREEN SEA TURTLE WINS!

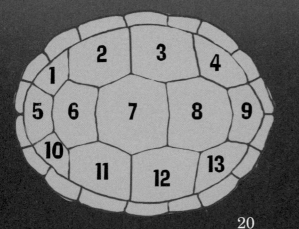

We started with 12 reptiles in round one. Now we've made it to the second round. Only 6 reptiles are left in this bracketed fight. After this round there will be three reptiles left.

Mambas are the fastest snakes in the world. This camouflaged mamba prefers to stay up in the trees where the leaves are green, just like its scales. It sees the chuckwalla and slithers down for a closer look.

ROUND 2 GREEN MAMBA VS. CHUCKWALLA MATCH 1

Chuckwallas are herbivores that eat flowers, leaves, and some fruits. They have no interest in eating green mambas. The chuckwalla sees the deadly green mamba.

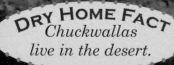

The chuckwalla sneaks into a crack and waits. When the green mamba snoops around, the chuckwalla stays motionless, hoping the snake will lose interest. The chuckwalla does not want to be eaten by the snake.

The chuckwalla expands his body. As he puffs up, a loose boulder falls and squishes the green mamba's head.

CHUCKWALLA WINS!

On to the next round!

The aggressive fer-de-lance is the deadliest snake in Central and South America. It causes more injuries than alligators and crocodiles. It ambushes small animals.

Watch out! Fer-de-lance! Danger! Scientists that study the rain forest have to be cautious around them.

FER-DE-LANCE VS. GAVIAL

The fish-eating gavial has interlocking teeth. It also has sharper teeth than a crocodile, alligator, or caiman. Gavials would not attack a human.

The fer-de-lance is an excellent swimmer. It swims
across a stream without knowing the gavial is
underwater patiently waiting for fish to swim by.

ZAP! The snake is mistaken for a fish and the
gavial slices the fer-de-lance before it even has a
chance to defend itself. The gavial is lucky. The
fer-de-lance did not have time to inject venom.

GAVIAL WINS!

If we wrote a *Most Dangerous Snake* book, the inland taipan would be number one. It is scary and nasty. So sorry, boomslang, cottonmouth, rattlesnake, sea snake, copperhead, king cobra, and puff adder, you all don't measure up. Turtles beware.

ROUND 2 — INLAND TAIPAN VS. GREEN SEA TURTLE — MATCH 3

A young green sea turtle will eat meat and fish. An adult green sea turtle eats seaweed and sea grass. The green sea turtle would have no interest in eating a snake. The green sea turtle is an herbivore.

DEFINITION
Herbivores eat plants.

SEA TURTLE FACT
There are 7 species of sea turtles: leatherback, green, hawksbill, Kemp's ridley, olive ridley, flatback, and loggerhead.

The inland taipan is from the inland desert. The green sea turtle is from the ocean. There are places on earth where the desert meets the ocean. The snake could never swallow a giant turtle. The green sea turtle shuffles ashore.

The inland taipan sees and smells the turtle. The two reptiles get close. The turtle senses the danger and goes back in the ocean and swims away.

The inland taipan wins and is going on to the finals.

INLAND TAIPAN WINS!

ROUND-ROBIN

Oh no! We started with 12 reptiles. Due to the math, there are only 3 reptiles left. In a bracketed tournament with 16 competitors we would have had THE REPTILE FINAL FOUR. We now need a round-robin type of championship finals.

We will use letters instead of numbers.

A	**B**	**C**
CHUCKWALLA	**GAVIAL**	**INLAND TAIPAN**

A will fight B, A will fight C. B will fight C. The reptile with the best record will win. May the best reptile win.

ROUND 3 — A CHUCKWALLA VS. B GAVIAL — MATCH 1

It's a lizard versus a crocodile type. A plant eater versus a fish eater. The chuckwalla has come a long way. Can it continue? The gavial has a tricky mouth and it could use its tail as a weapon.

DENTAL FACT
Some gavials have 100 teeth.

27

The smaller chuckwalla doesn't stand a chance. How cou[ld]
it fight the larger gavial? Puffing itself up will not work.

The gavial uses its tail like a whip.

SMACK!

GAVIAL WINS!

In a round-robin, both contestants have to fight again.
Rest up, chuckwalla.

The chuckwalla recovered from the first fight and now faces the inland taipan. It is not looking good for the chuckwalla.

ROUND 3 — A CHUCKWALLA VS. C INLAND TAIPAN — MATCH 2

It's lizard versus snake. Four legs versus no legs. No poison versus venom. Teeth versus fangs.

The chuckwalla trots away from the inland taipan. The snake follows. The inland taipan strikes. Ouch! Its fangs pierce the chuckwalla and the inland taipan injects venom. The fight is over.

INLAND TAIPAN WINS!

Good night, chuckwalla, you are out! There is one fight left.

FINAL MATCH!

Both reptiles have won a match in the round-robin. This fight will settle it all. The winner will be champion of the Ultimate Reptile Rumble.

	WINS	LOSSES
GAVIAL	1	0
INLAND TAIPAN	1	0
CHUCKWALLA	0	2

ROUND **3**

B GAVIAL VS. C INLAND TAIPAN

MATCH **3**

This fight is sharp teeth, teeth, and more teeth versus deadly venom. Four legs versus no legs. Crocodilia versus serpentes.

CLASSIFICATION FACT
Crocodiles, alligators, caimans, and gavials are in a group called crocodilia.

SERPENTES
Scientific classification of snakes.

The gavial sees the inland taipan. The snake would love to slither over and put its fangs into the gavial. The snake is too slow. The gavial quickly turns its head and one of its teeth smacks the inland taipan. The snake is wounded.

GAVIAL WINS!

This is one way the competition might have ended. Write your own ending or think of a new version of an Ultimate Rumble book.